THE
BIG
TIME

ALEX MORGAN

LAURA K. MURRAY

CREATIVE EDUCATION

ALEX MORGAN

TABLE OF CONTENTS

Meet Alex	**5**
Alex's Childhood	**9**
Getting into Soccer	**11**
The Big Time	**15**
Off the Field	**19**
What Is Next?	**21**
What Alex Says About ...	**23**

Glossary	Read More	Websites	Index
24	**24**	**24**	**24**

MEET ALEX

Alex dribbles down the field. She cuts toward the goal. She kicks the ball into the corner of the net. Goal! The crowd goes wild! Fans wave signs with the number 13.

Alex Morgan is a professional soccer player. She is a *forward* with the Portland Thorns FC. She is a speedy goalscorer. Many people think she is one of the best soccer players today!

Alex started playing for the Oregon team in 2013.

ALEX'S CHILDHOOD

Alex was born July 2, 1989. She grew up in Diamond Bar, California. Her full name is Alex-andra. She has two older sisters named Jeni and Jeri. As a child, Alex was fast!

Alex and her mom, Pamela.

DIAMOND BAR, CALIFORNIA

GETTING INTO SOCCER

Alex started playing soccer at age 14. Alex ran track and played volleyball, too. She hurt her right knee in high school. But she worked hard to get healthy.

After high school, Alex made sure she always stretched before playing.

Alex played college soccer for the University of California, Berkeley. She had 45 goals in college. In 2008, Alex played on the *U-20* women's national team for the United States. She kept playing for the U.S. at the 2011 FIFA Women's World Cup.

Alex became the youngest member of the U.S. women's national team in 2009.

THE BIG TIME

In 2011, Alex was *drafted* by a pro team, the Western New York Flash. The Flash won the league championship that year. Then Alex joined the Seattle Sounders Women.

Alex was the first Women's Professional Soccer draft pick in 2011.

Alex was named the U.S. Soccer Female Athlete of the Year in 2012. She and the U.S. women's team went to the 2012 Summer Olympics. They won the gold medal! In 2013, Alex joined the Portland Thorns FC. The club is based in Oregon.

. . . .

Alex and Olympic teammate Megan Rapinoe showed off their gold medals.

OFF THE FIELD

In her free time, Alex reads and does *yoga*. She runs soccer camps for kids. She even wrote a children's book series called *The Kicks*. In 2014, Alex married fellow pro soccer player Servando Carrasco.

. . . .

Alex and Servando got married on New Year's Eve in California.

WHAT IS NEXT?

Alex planned to keep playing all over the world. She traveled to Canada for the 2015 Women's World Cup. She got ready for the 2016 Summer Olympics, too. Those Games were held in Brazil. Alex's fans were excited to cheer her on!

In 2015, Alex helped the U.S. national team win the Women's World Cup.

WHAT ALEX SAYS ABOUT ...

ATTITUDE

"There are certain things you can control in life, and your attitude is a big one."

BEING A ROLE MODEL

"I want to show girls that their dreams can become a reality through believing in yourself and being confident in everything you do."

PENALTY KICKS

"I ... stare at the ball, follow through, and never look at the place that I'm going to shoot."

GLOSSARY

drafted picked to be on a team; in a sports draft, teams take turns choosing players

forward in soccer, a player who stays close to the other team's goal and has more chances to score

U-20 in soccer, this means "under 20 years old"

yoga an activity that involves stretching and breathing

READ MORE

Murray, Laura K. *Cristiano Ronaldo*. Mankato, Minn.: Creative Education, 2017.

Wendorff, Anne. *Soccer*. Minneapolis: Bellwether Media, 2010.

WEBSITES

Alex Morgan Profile

http://www.ussoccer.com/players/2014/03/15/02/36 /alex-morgan

Learn more about Alex on the U.S. Soccer site.

Alex Morgan Soccer

http://www.alexmorgansoccer.com/

This is Alex's own site, with photos, videos, and more.

INDEX

awards 16
Carrasco, Servando 19
childhood 9, 11
college 12
Diamond Bar, California 9
family 9, 19
interests 11, 19
Olympics 16, 21
Portland Thorns FC 7, 16
pro teams 7, 15, 16
U.S. national teams 12, 16, 21

PUBLISHED BY Creative Education
P.O. Box 227, Mankato, Minnesota 56002
Creative Education is an imprint of The Creative Company
www.thecreativecompany.us

DESIGN AND PRODUCTION BY Christine Vanderbeek
ART DIRECTION BY Rita Marshall
PRINTED IN the United States of America

PHOTOGRAPHS BY Alamy (Jonathan Larsen/Diadem Images), Corbis (Bob Daemmrich/Bob Daemmrich Photography, Inc., Thomas Eisenhuth/isiphotos.com, J. Adam Fenster/isiphotos.com, Rolf Kosecki, Craig Mitchelldyer/ISI, Anne M. Peterson/AP, Howard C. Smith/ISI, John Todd/ISI), Getty Images (Brian Bahr/Stringer, Handout/Handout), iStockphoto (Pingebat), photosinbox.com

LIBRARY OF CONGRESS CATALOGING-IN-PUBLICATION DATA
Murray, Laura K.
Alex Morgan / Laura K. Murray.
p. cm. — (The big time)
Includes index.
Summary: An elementary introduction to the life, work, and popularity of Alex Morgan, an American soccer star who helped the U.S. women's soccer team win gold in the 2012 Summer Olympics.

ISBN 978-1-60818-667-9 (HARDCOVER)
ISBN 978-1-56660-703-2 (EBOOK)
1. Morgan, Alex (Alexandra Patricia), 1989–Juvenile literature. 2. Soccer players—United States—Biography—Juvenile literature.
GV942.7.M673 M87 2016
796.334092—dc23   2015026250

CCSS: RI.1.1, 2, 3, 4, 5, 6, 7; RI.2.1, 2, 5, 6, 7; RI.3.1, 5, 7, 8; RI.4.3, 5; RF.1.1, 3, 4; RF.2.3, 4

FIRST EDITION 9 8 7 6 5 4 3 2 1